THE GREAT FESTIVAL OF THE MARDI GRAS

HOLIDAY BOOKS FOR CHILDREN

Children's Holiday Books

BABY PROFESSOR

EDUCATION KIDS

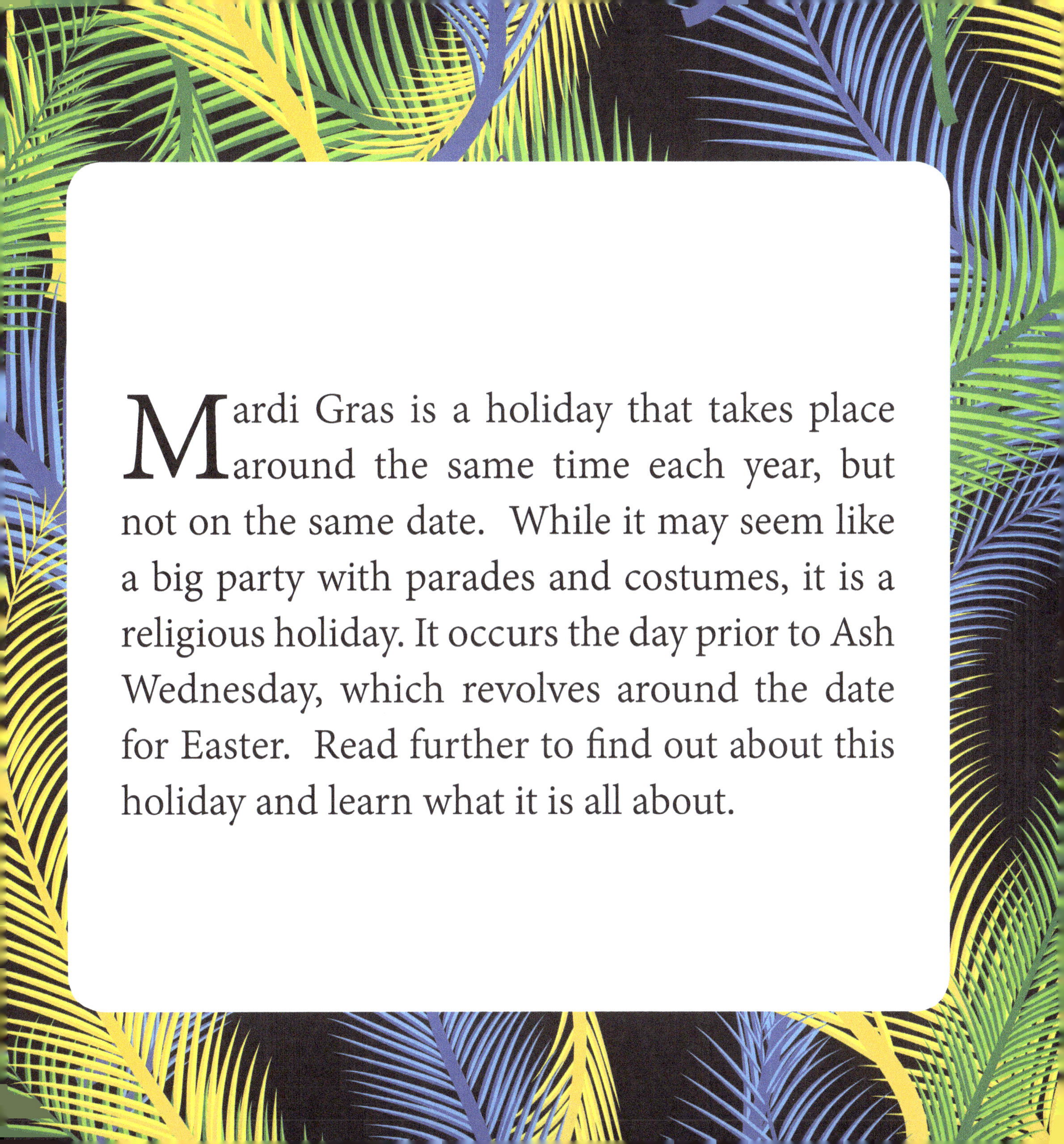

Mardi Gras is a holiday that takes place around the same time each year, but not on the same date. While it may seem like a big party with parades and costumes, it is a religious holiday. It occurs the day prior to Ash Wednesday, which revolves around the date for Easter. Read further to find out about this holiday and learn what it is all about.

WHAT DOES IT CELEBRATE?

It occurs on the last day of the carnival, and it occurs the day prior Ash Wednesday, which is the beginning of the Christian season known as Lent. It refers to the events of Carnival celebrations, which begin or after the feasts of Epiphany (Three Kings Day) and concluding the day prior to Ash Wednesday. The term Mardi Gras means "Fat Tuesday" in French, which is where the practice of eating the fatty, richer foods before Lent begins.

Some related practices associate with the Shrovetide celebration which occurs prior to the religious and fasting obligations which are associated with the penitential Lent season.

In England, for example, is where it is known as Shrove Tuesday, which derives from the term shrive which means confess.

Some of the other names are Tuesday of Carnival and Pancake Day. England celebrates Pancake Day, where it was quite common to use up the butter, milk, and eggs before Ash Wednesday. These were the ingredients that were often used in making pancakes.

WHEN IS IT CELEBRATED?

It always occurs the day prior to Ash Wednesday. Since Ash Wednesday moves with Easter, the Mardi Gras date moves with it. Listed below are past and future Mardi Gras dates:

- February 21, 2012
- February 12, 2013
- March 4, 2014
- February 17, 2015

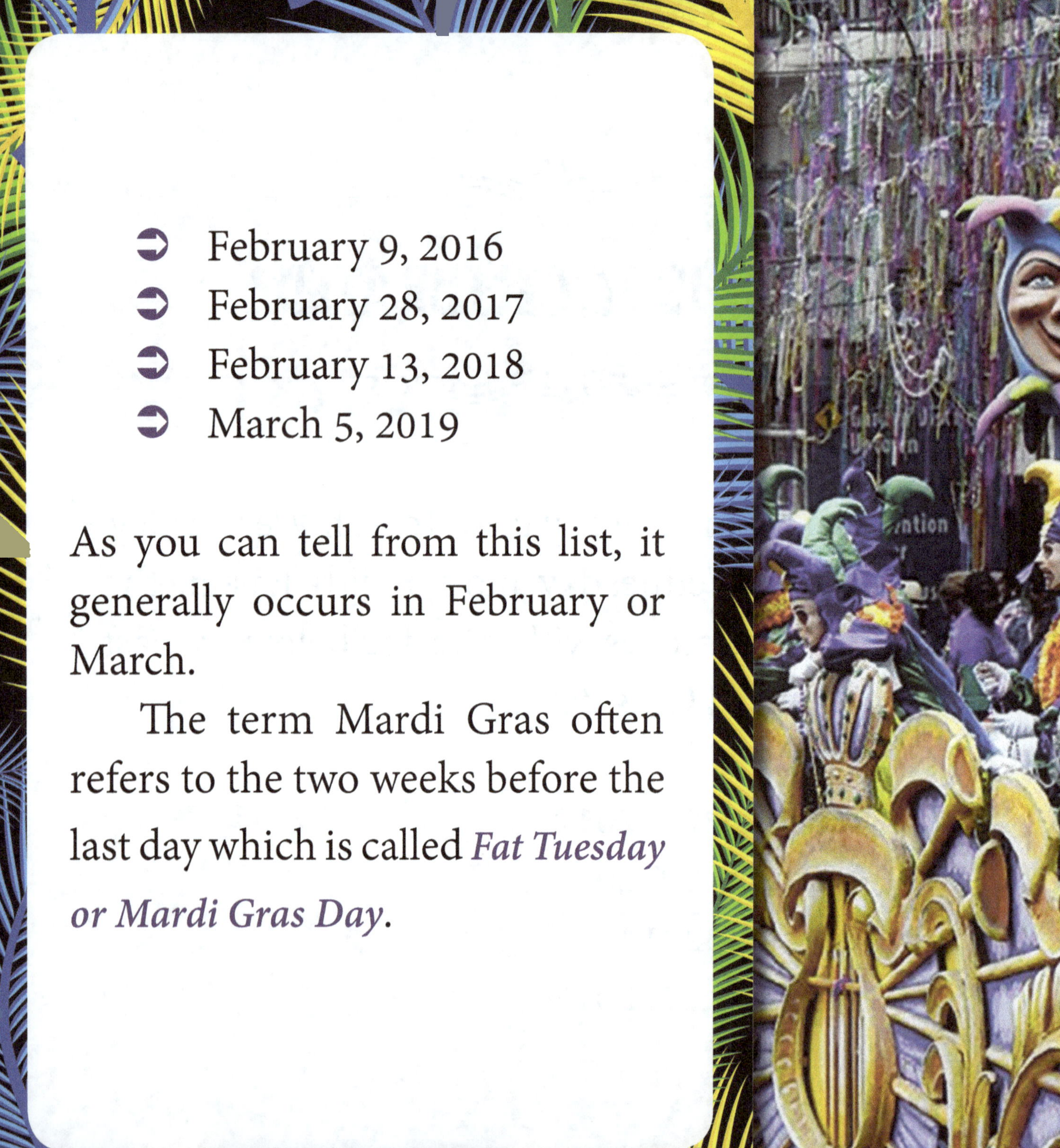

- February 9, 2016
- February 28, 2017
- February 13, 2018
- March 5, 2019

As you can tell from this list, it generally occurs in February or March.

The term Mardi Gras often refers to the two weeks before the last day which is called *Fat Tuesday or Mardi Gras Day*.

3
The King's
Jesters

WHO CELEBRATES IT?

Celebrations are held all over the world. It is an official holiday in Louisiana, and celebrated by lots of people. Many see it as a reason to enjoy a great party, especially in New Orleans. Some of the more noted celebrations are held in the French settled areas, specifically in Louisiana and in the city of New Orleans.

HOW IS IT CELEBRATED?

Many cities in the United States celebrate with a parade, with the greatest celebration taking place in New Orleans, Louisiana. There will be marching bands and colorful floats in the parade and people will dress in crazy and bright costumes.

They also celebrate with dances, or balls. Some are known as masquerade balls and people dress in masks and costumes so people won't know who they are.

Items are tossed from the floats into the crowds. These include colorful beads and doubloons, which are toy coins. Krewes are the private clubs organizing the parades and events in New Orleans.

Many people celebrate by hosting or attending a king cake party. This is a cake similar to a coffee cake that has a bead or figurine baked inside. It is tradition that whoever finds the bead then had to host the next king cake party.

TRADITIONS IN OTHER COUNTRIES

Belgium

It is one of the most significant days during the year in Binche, Belgium and is the peak of the Carnival of Binche. Thousands of Gilles dance to traditional carnival songs around city starting in the morning and dancing past dusk.

Brazil

Carnival is the most celebrated Brazilian holiday. Brazil will attract 70% of its tourists during this celebration. While variations in their celebration are held in the various cities of Brazil, the same is incorporated to each of them.

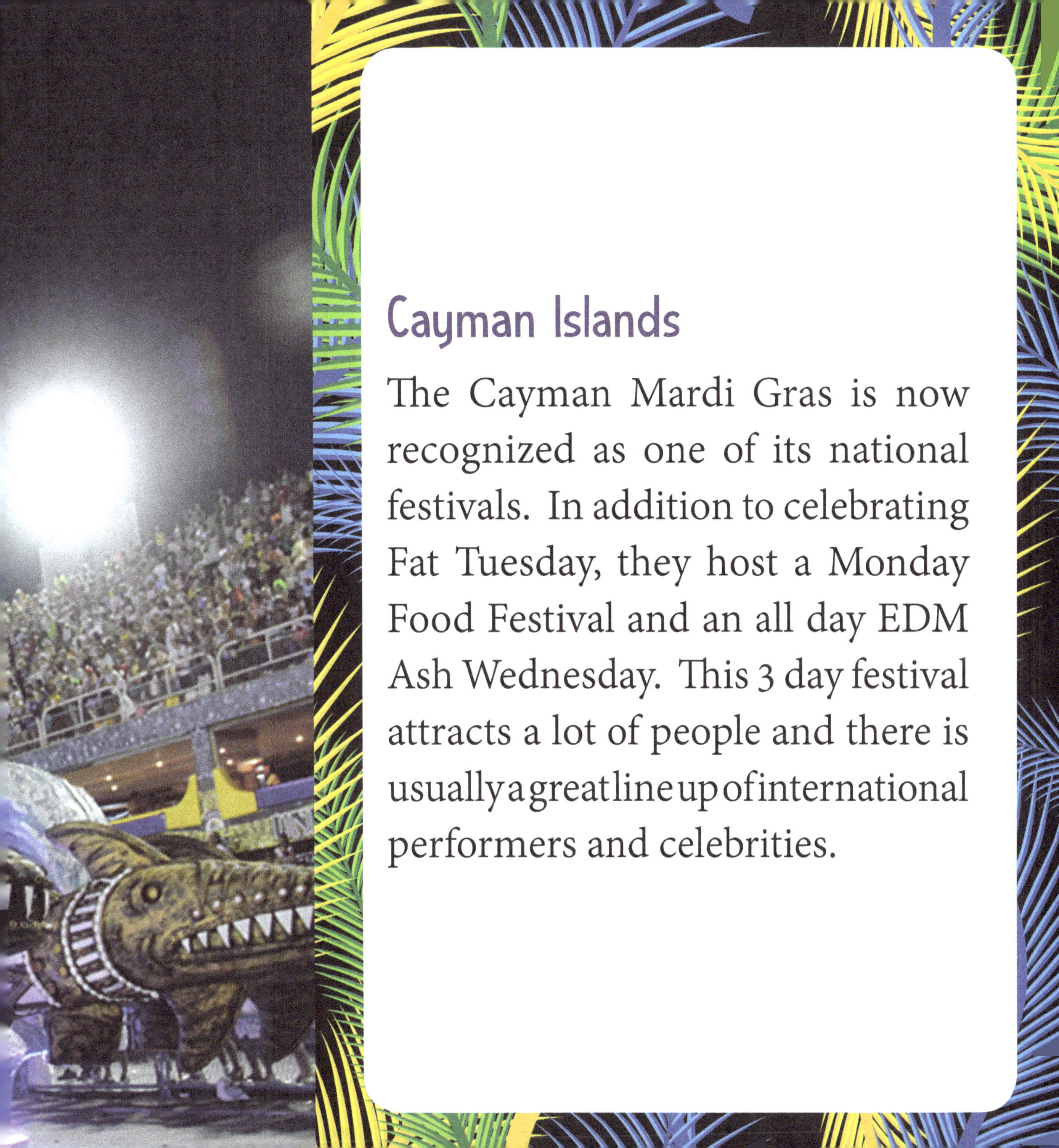

Cayman Islands

The Cayman Mardi Gras is now recognized as one of its national festivals. In addition to celebrating Fat Tuesday, they host a Monday Food Festival and an all day EDM Ash Wednesday. This 3 day festival attracts a lot of people and there is usually a great line up of international performers and celebrities.

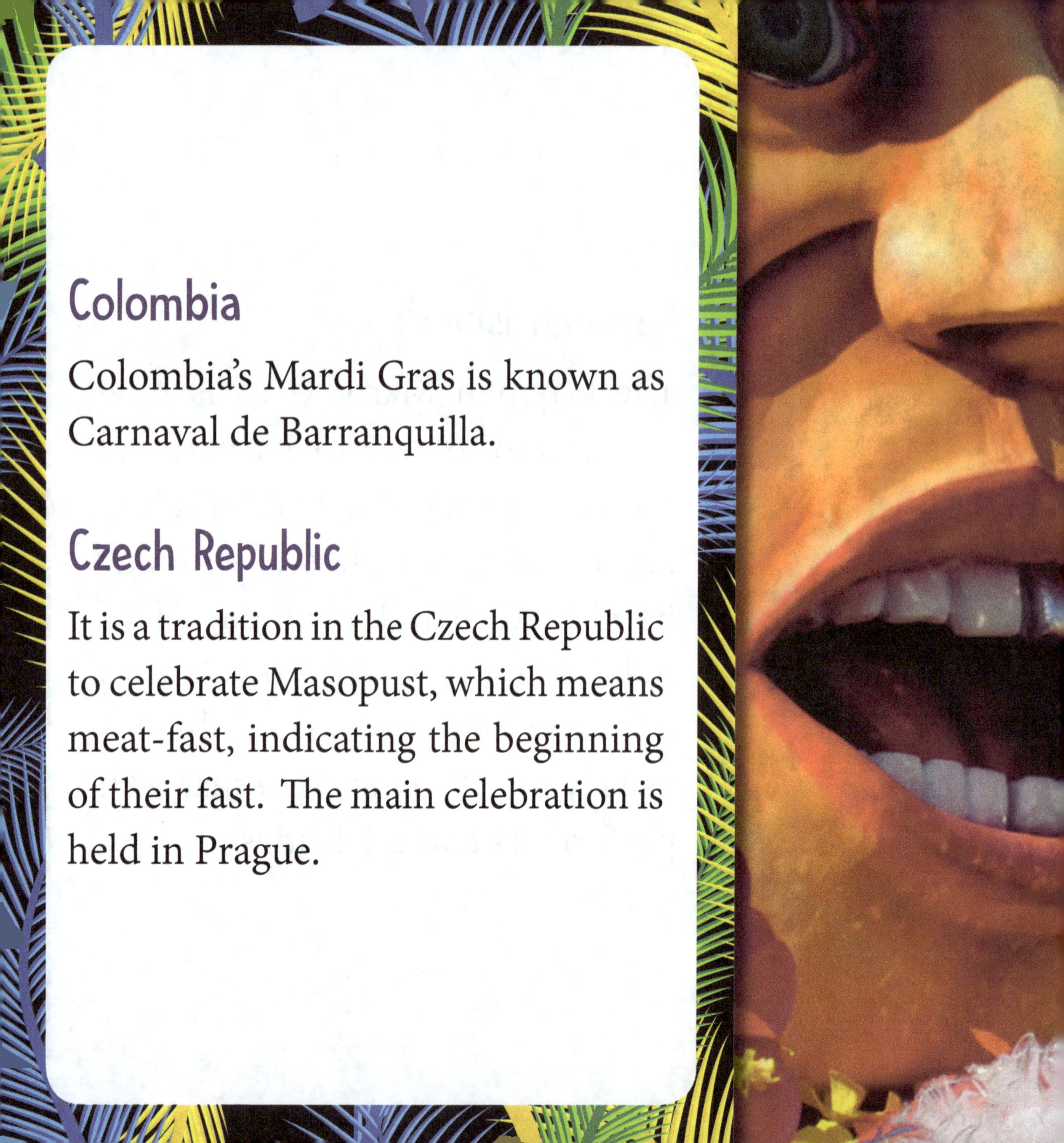

Colombia

Colombia's Mardi Gras is known as Carnaval de Barranquilla.

Czech Republic

It is a tradition in the Czech Republic to celebrate Masopust, which means meat-fast, indicating the beginning of their fast. The main celebration is held in Prague.

REIN
CAPITANA PRE-
María Luisa De
Brilla
Brilla

Germany

In Germany, the celebration is held on the same day but goes by many names, including Fetter Donnerstog (Fat Tuesday), Unsinniger Donnerstag, Greesentag, Weiberfastnacht, among other. They are typically only a part of the entire event which occurs one or sometimes two weeks prior to Ash Wednesday.

Italy

Mardi Gras is known as Martedi Grasso (Fat Tuesday) in Italy. It is the key day of Carnival and with the Thursday that falls before, is called Giovedi Grasso (Fat Thursday), which designates the beginning of the celebrations.

The most renowned Carnivals take place in Ivrea, Viareggio, and Venice. The "Battle of Oranges" takes place in Ivrea.

Netherlands

A festival that is similar to Mardi Gras takes place in the Netherlands. It goes by the name Carnaval. The word Carnaval originates from carnem levare which means "to take away meat" in Latin. This marks the start of Lent which leads to Easter.

Sweden

The celebration in Sweden goes by the name Fettisdagen, when you eat fastiagsbulle, often referred to as Semla. The name arises from "fett" (fat) and "tisday" (Tuesday). In the beginning, this day was the only one when you should eat fastlagsbullar.

As you can tell, although they celebrate in many different ways, they are very similar.

HISTORY

Its history can be tracked as far back as the Middle Ages. It was during these times that people would eat heartily the night prior to beginning their fast on Ash Wednesday.

Other similar traditions began occurring during the Middle Ages which includes the 12th century France tradition of serving the king's cake.

In the early times in England, this day was known as a religious day when a person would confess their sins in preparation for Lent.

On March 2, 1699, French-Canadian explorer Jean Baptiste Le Moyne Sieur de Bienville landed south of New Orleans.

Since this was the evening prior to Mardi Gras, he called this landing point as "Point du Mardi Gras". It was first celebrated in 1703 at a small settlement in Fort Louis de la Mobile. It was in the 1730s that Mardi Gras then became a popular New Orleans celebration.

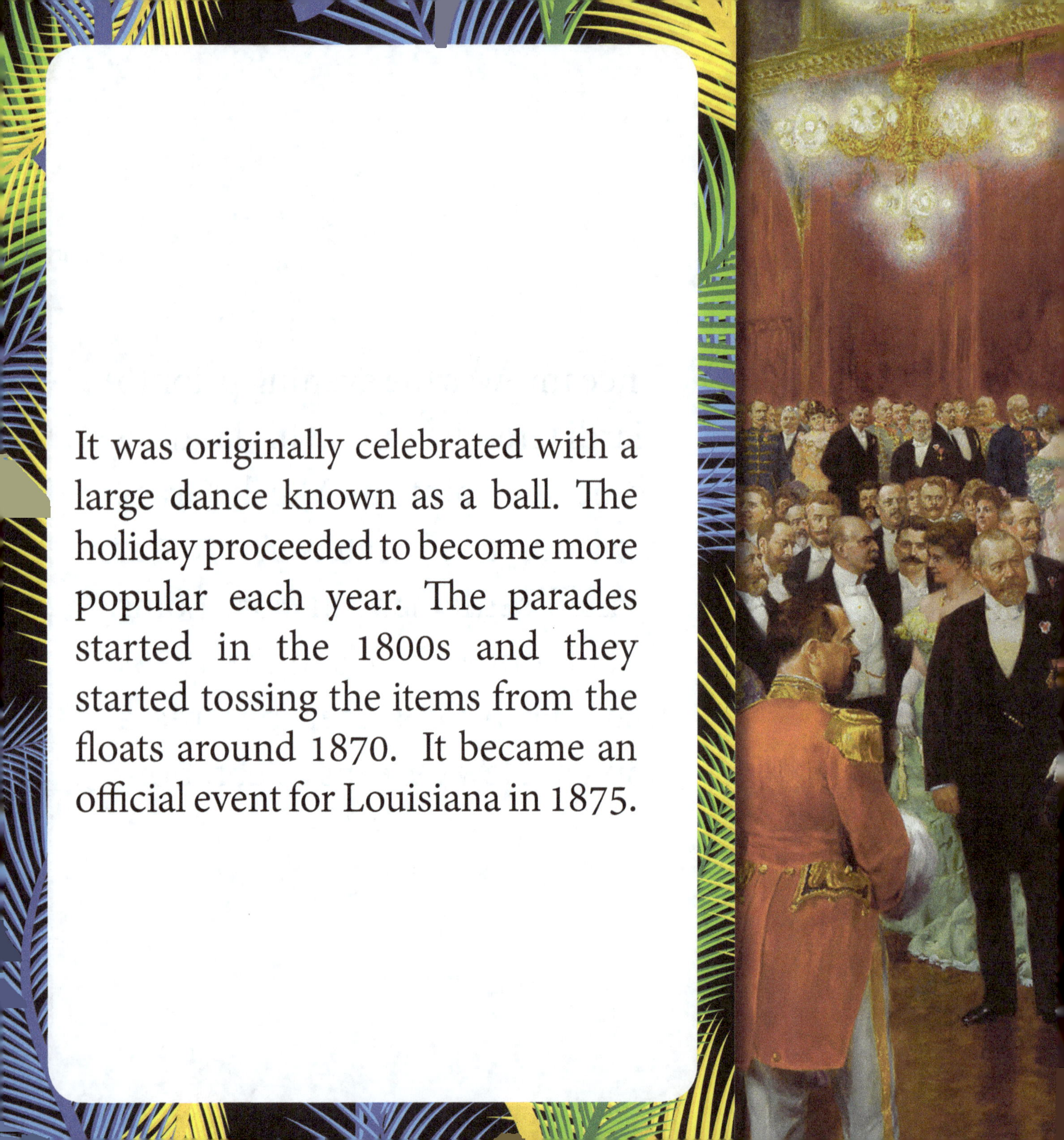

It was originally celebrated with a large dance known as a ball. The holiday proceeded to become more popular each year. The parades started in the 1800s and they started tossing the items from the floats around 1870. It became an official event for Louisiana in 1875.

This is the Tuesday prior to Ash Wednesday and is also known to be Mardi Gras Day and Shrove Day. On this day, people eat all the food they want since the next day is Ash Wednesday, the beginning of Lent, a time of fasting for Christians. Christians also have to give up something else they enjoy for this period of time. Fat Tuesday is considered a celebration and opportunity to enjoy something that you will be giving up for Lent.

THE BRIGHT COLORS

Purple, gold, and green are the official colors of the holiday. The purple represents justice, gold represents power, and green represents faith. Most of the costumes, as well as the beads and other trinkets, will be made using these colors. You will also sometimes find these colors on top of the king cake.

ASH WEDNESDAY

It is known as a Christian holiday. It is the beginning of Lent, which, not counting Sundays, is 40 days spent fasting and in repentance before Easter. Ash Wednesday occurs 46 days prior to Easter. As with Mardi Gras, as the date for Easter moves around, Ash Wednesday does as well. February 4th is the earliest that it can occur with the latest day being March 10th.

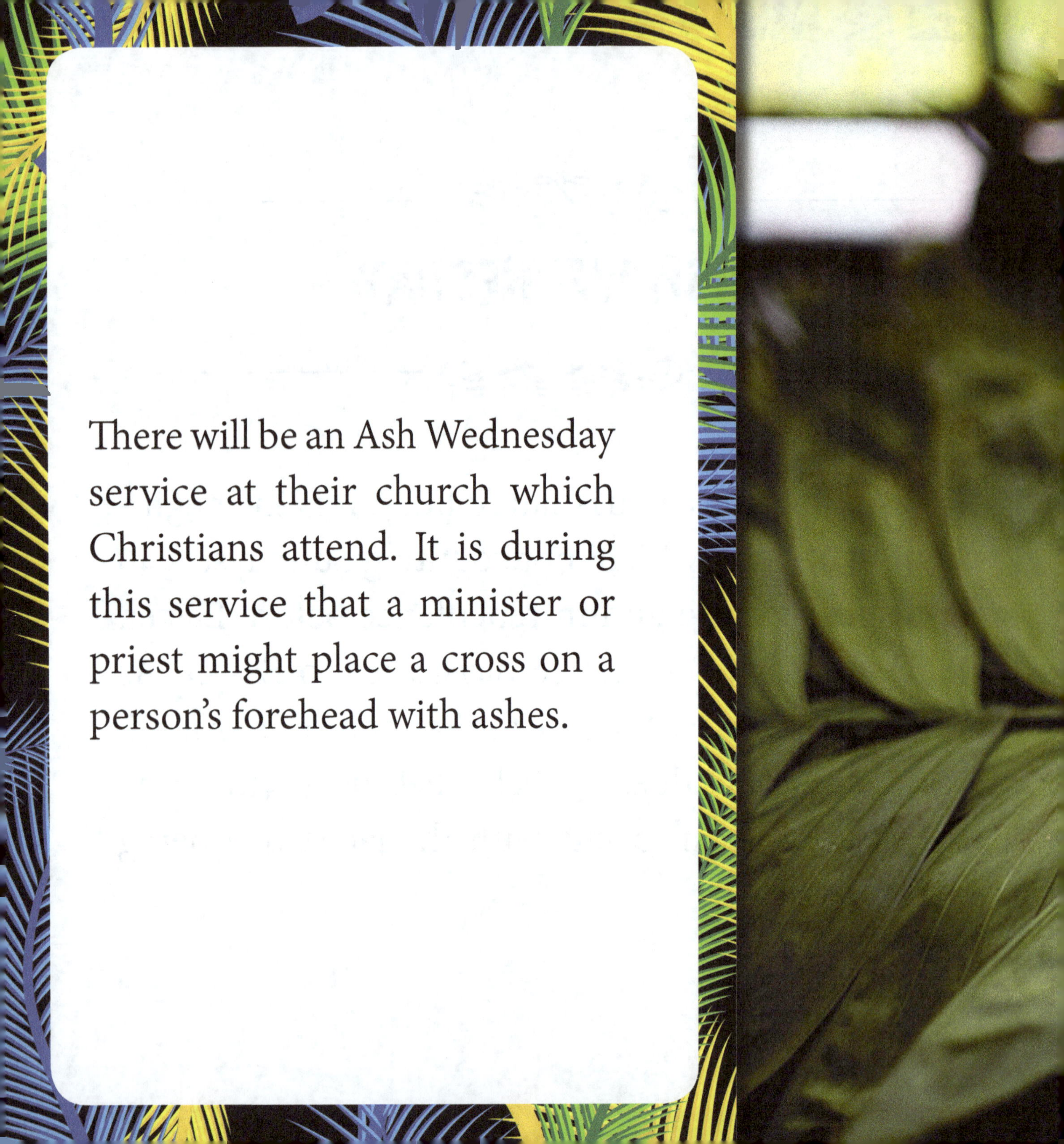

There will be an Ash Wednesday service at their church which Christians attend. It is during this service that a minister or priest might place a cross on a person's forehead with ashes.

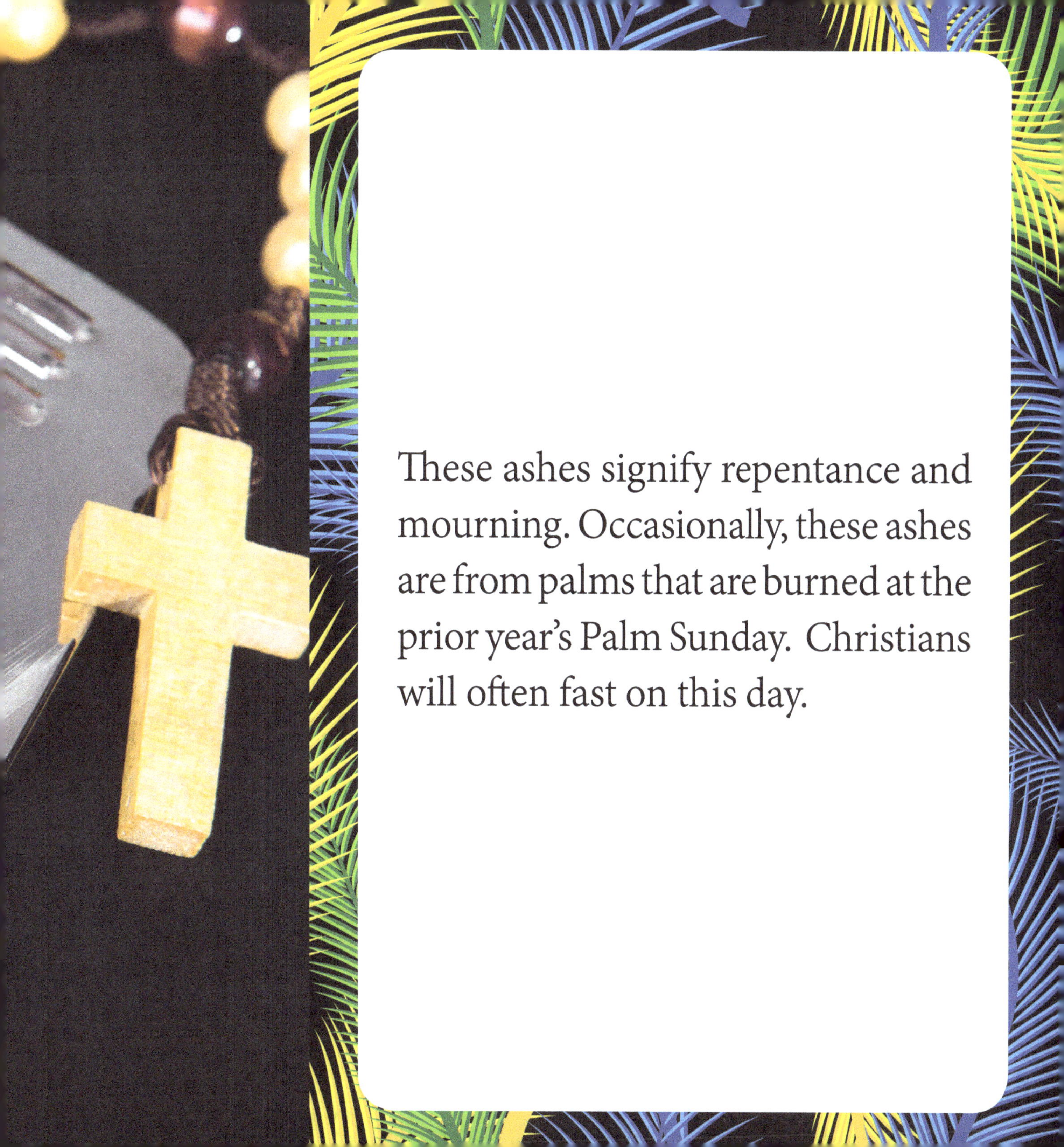

These ashes signify repentance and mourning. Occasionally, these ashes are from palms that are burned at the prior year's Palm Sunday. Christians will often fast on this day.

While they are permitted to eat one meal or two small meals, many choose to fast throughout the day with only water and bread. They do not eat any meat on this day. Fasting can continue during Lent and in particular on Good Friday.

Christians also will give up something as a sacrifice or offer. This might be in the form of a particular food, such as chocolate, video games, and even using hot water for a shower.

Be sure to research additional information about Mardi Gras by researching the internet, going to your local library, or asking questions of your teachers, family, and friends.

Visit

BABY PROFESSOR
EDUCATION KIDS

www.BabyProfessorBooks.com
to download Free Baby Professor eBooks
and view our catalog of new and exciting
Children's Books